Dancing
in the Cobwebs

poems by

Dom Fonce

Finishing Line Press
Georgetown, Kentucky

Dancing
in the Cobwebs

For Hanna Sassya
I love and miss you.

ACKNOWLEDGMENTS

Grateful acknowledgment to the journals in which these poems first appeared:

Blacklist Journal: "For the Puffer Fish"
Delmarva Review: "Song for the Wild Frog"
Obra/Artifact: "Grassman"
Ohio's Best Emerging Poets 2019: An Anthology: "Thick with Howl"
Rappahannock Review: "Dancing in the Cobwebs"
Sweet Tree Review: "The Fair"
Unlost Journal: "The Great Man"
The Weekly Degree: "Beetle Song;" "Song for George"
West Texas Literary Review: "Nowhere-Man"
The Write Launch: "She said, 'Let go—I'm a memory. I'm not real.'"; "She said, 'Lift;'" "Song for Circe"

Publisher: Leah Huete de Maines
Editor: Christen Kincaid
Cover Art: Allison Janicki
Author Photo: Sadie George-Pasquale Photography, LLC
Cover Design: Elizabeth Maines McCleavy

Order online: www.finishinglinepress.com
also available on amazon.com

Author inquiries and mail orders:
Finishing Line Press
PO Box 1626
Georgetown, Kentucky 40324
USA

Table of Contents

Dancing in the Cobwebs

Grandpa built the coffee table from empty
packs, painted the popcorn ceiling
yellow with smoke. With shaking hands,
eyes rolled back, a stale cigarette
reached its end like the fuse on a dud.

Past the pill bottles, the cold cups
of coffee, we saw the crumpled carton.

Pop, pop, pop! John Wayne shot
from the hip between Grandpa's snores.

We heard the gunfire echo
into the back field, took
one of his Camels each, escaping
the sunlight in our fort.
Unlit, they hung from our lips
as we danced in the cobwebs.

My sister put tea on the plastic stove.
I drank whiskey from an empty bottle.
Look, I'm Grandpa! I said,
gulping sunflower seeds, slumping
over in my seat,
eyes closed.

Look, I'm a cowboy!
my sister yelled, hand now a gun
pointed at my chest.
Our mouths switched between laughter
and *pew-pew* noises. In the distance,

a massive shot turned us to stone.
Through the cloth door, we saw
a deer—ghost-white with red eyes—
stumble in the grass.
A yelp.
A second bang.
We tossed the cigarettes,
ran into the house.
The sky swelling, blackening,
prepared to cry with us.

Grandpa's Men

We rolled in ditches, swung on every branch,
as broken cars rumbled towards our house.

The passenger seats showed the scowls of men
who looked like blackflies smelling rot. A moth,

with crystal wings and bulbous eyes, hovered
in honeysuckle—up and down, I trailed

it through the grass and past the house I saw
a face inside. His eyes fell back like trees

decaying in the rain. The men came in;
the men came out, transforming every time.

You think they come for help? my sister said.
Maybe, I replied. *Grandpa fixes them.*

And when the final man had left, we went
inside to see if everything was fine.

The dark had eaten Grandpa whole and he
had lain there motionless. *Are you okay?*

He struggled upright, walked right out the door.
We watched him in the back—without a thought

he jumped into the pond and blasted out:
I hate this skin. I need to wash myself!

Litany

Frost-breath hanging from a tongue,
when I was young, mother-breath had been flung
at me, for my child-breath from child lungs had sprung.

Burning-breath hanging from a tongue,
when I was young, the tea kettle sung
and on my eager mouth it stung.

Lithe-breath hanging from a tongue,
when I was young, a cardinal fluttered among
the leaves and near the sun he hung.

Black-breath hanging from a tongue,
though I am old, my father is still young
for in his youth his fate had been unstrung.

Song for the Wild Frog

We pinned you to a tree
while the adults watched television—

your underside, the softest
parts, yawning
at our fingertips.

We remembered the cartoons,
the gross-out humor, the frog

splayed open on
steel, and the kids, much older
than ourselves, holding distaste and curiosity

simultaneously in each eye—and we looked
at you, muscle
trying to jump through skin,
without pleasure, without humor,
without a sense of purpose at all,

and we cut deeply down your belly.

In there, in you, was something
new to my young, naïve mind—pain
created by me.

You winced like a man
trapped in a fire, and we
let you fall to the grass, ran back inside
and hid in our rooms.

When we were called for supper, we ate our words instead,
and at night we sat underneath
our covers with flashlights—

the ghost of you smeared on our walls.

In the morning, we collected you

from the dirt, and held you tight,
                              like a lost toy.

                    The brown earth ate our
hands as we scooped out a place for you.
     We called it the "Frog Spot" and, as play came,

              as seasons changed, our feet
dodged your grave, as if it were a
                              landmine.

House Sonnet

The house is haunted with the feet of boys
who sleep in crawlspaces like Dad when he

was young. On summer days, I can recall
my father throwing me into pillars

of hay, his job when he was twelve—the way
he paid for lunch at school. The scratchy straw

still prickles at my thighs. The kitchen's packed
with Grandpa's snores as Grandma cries herself

to sleep, but in the attic Dad remains,
a ghost that's lost in time. Every August

he reappears to feel the hardwood floor
and wager marbles with me in a pile.

When I ask him if he remembers me
he shakes his head and looks into his hands.

The Great Man: A Found Poem

*Source: Dozens of sympathy cards sent
to my family after my father's death.*

I was thinking of the world
and the men that leave their mark on it—
the way they live their lives. Fathers
like Gods to their children, their loved ones.
Be a sorry man and it's your loss; be a great man
and soon face great death like a great man, early,
with your children together, mourning,
and your heart quiet, but strong. The sorry man,
the little man, is a garden of maybe and somehow—
                                        no, that's not you.

Don't turn out like that, Dominic. Please take care
to be just like your father.

For the Puffer Fish

Males laboriously flap their fins as they
swim along the seafloor, resulting in
disrupted sediment and amazing circular patterns.
—article on puffer fish sand art

Yes, I've placed the breath
of a woman
on my tongue and wanted more—to shape
earth with the breeze
collected in my lungs—craved
the attention, ballooning my chest
as I walked.

I understand, puffer fish, signals
and symbols can be lifted, offered,
and smoothed down to nothing
in a blink—bodies sprawled on a bed,
digging burial mounds into the sheets
that evaporate in the morning light. But failure is a basket
holding spurned cockles, sheddings, to flatten
and paint on next.

In the winter, my father blew
fumes from his nose onto
the frozen window—wrote
love letters to my mother
in spilled coffee grounds. In death, he etched chicken scratch
into the ether
as soul twirled through dust.
And she, his woman, sat rock-heavy in his hand.

She marked his patterns with her own—water
seeping into deadwood—tied his thumbs
to the bed and wailed on his torso, trying
to blanket his ghost.

And this weight is worth dancing
and painting over, puffer fish.
It is always worth it.

Pixie Sonnet

When it was hot and I was skipping stones,
I met a redhead in a daze. She laughed

and held her nose, then threw one twice as far.
Approaching her, she turned to run away.

Until she stopped and threw her lips at mine.
Her hands then passed to smoke and at the edge

of water my eyes landed on the waves—
reflections held her smile in the trees

and out her back had sprouted shining wings.
She fluttered branch to branch, my name hovered

in my ear. I asked her, *What does this mean?*
She said, *The air is sweet with marigold*

and what you've asked for can't be told.
And so she left and never did return.

She said, "Let go—I'm a memory. I'm not real."

I've counted every single hair
you left in my room, gathered
them up, and scattered them
in the grass. It is not enough

to wash away the blood;
the wood must be burned too—
each carpet fiber must be picked,
each nail lifted, each floorboard

taken to the pile. Everything you
touched and touched you, smells
and tastes of you, will be eaten
by the sky. In the end, I reshape

matter and mass in the yard. I'm
mad, making an effigy in the dirt—
my last good look at you—and digging
for roots, anything that will keep me

tethered. Anything is a ritual if prayer
comes before practice. I cut off
the swath of me that was taken when we
lay in bed, fantasizing a future

that failed to materialize. It is okay.
Earth will retake her ashes—us too
in time—but no memory is tangible
and whenever I try to pin it down,

the location thins to clouds
in my grasps. You are unobtainable,
anima trapped inside a bottle, and the lid
burrows into me with each twist.

Song for George

Our deepest fears are like dragons, guarding our deepest treasure.
—Rainer Maria Rilke

The roads were gravel, pill bottles
chimed in the wind, and I was
an 8-year-old given the latchkey, free

to make mud castles in the yard and catch
frogs under my shirt. Cousin George—high
and brain-fried—played too, moved

his old Cavalier out back and shot at it
with a rifle all day long as if tomorrow
made a promise never to come. He cursed

his hands whenever it jammed, his voice
as coarse as a stone swirling in a coffee tin.
I watched his muscles spasm with each sprung

casing, the dangling Newports ashing themselves
off his lips. I gathered his beer cans like fallen
coins and stacked them in the woods, thinking

the meager droplets left behind were elixir
on my tongue, then stole the BB gun
from the neighbor's shed—in this fantasy, I was sure

I was drunk and dangerous like him, I was a ball
of fire like him. From a distance, the bangs echoed
in my ears, as I flung the cans into the air, picking

them off while they hovered within the clouds. Between
each massive bang, my small ting mimicked in turn—big,
small—until a stray dropped a cardinal, soft

as a pillow, from a tree. It flapped, squirmed,
and squawked as blood rushed into its lungs. With leaking
palms, I pumped five times and popped it from its suffering, staring

down at its lifelessness, blinking three times, not knowing
what else to do, not understanding why the air
around me fell as silent as a ghost-touched heartbeat.

Sister Sonnet

Your hand led me away from Grandpa's screams—
in dreams you said that underneath a rock

a tunnel opened to a darkened world,
that we could fall and drift in nothingness

like foaming suds that phantom down a drain.
I said the house is haunted, the woods shake,

can this really be the escape we need?
She said there is only one way to know,

so jump once for a blank slate, jump twice for
rebirth—reshape our mother's womb—just jump

for weightlessness and let the worry hang
among the leaves, we'll be free as the birds.

The stone left our feet as we spun like tops
just before mud ate our milky bodies.

Bags (and What They Hold)

In the bags underneath her eyes, my mother
cushioned us like tadpoles, moth-dust
soft. In our dreams, the night sky was a sack
of marbles—our father poked

the reddest light: *Now look through the eyepiece. That's*
Mars—

and we felt the warm
pap of sand swallow our toes.

In our waking, his photo
leans on a pile of ashes, ghosts swirling
in his painted eyes. We are infantile still, looking for promise, an
ear to a swollen
womb, but there is nothing left hiding
under the cinder blocks—he is gone, and the stars are colliding.

Our mother knows this, sees our aimless faces and puts
them in her pocket, as we jingle on her skin barefoot.

Thick with Howl

I sag
           to the floor
every time I'm in the hallway, when a sob

           ghosts through the walls of your room.
                      On these nights, the air is thick

           with howl, and I cup my ears, listening
                      to you, my mother,
     in cosmic conversation
                with my father.

           The silver lines from
     your eyes are sweet and palpable—the scent
                will always attract his kind.

           Here, you turn wedding vows into opera intonations
that dance butter-soft in the sheets: to hear his voice again, to catch

           the two of you in tandem—recreating
                      what placed you into the world together—strikes me
black.

           My profile will always melt through the doorway

     on nights like these. I'm a ritual. It's necessary

                I become toothless
           and begin mewling within the carpet fiber, small
as lint, and cut into
                      the chirpy swaying and singing—

Here, I'm three again, pulling
on your pant leg or disrupting lovemaking
by bursting onto the bed, kicking
at a dream,
birthing your chastity.

Can you hear the shrieking maws
rumpet the song of gone, the poltergeist-ing
waltz, bones in pirouette? You, my father. Can you hear
me shaking?

I'm the innocence
of fresh skin

on pavement.

I'm the child-breath
that asks what it means
to "be dead."

I'm the overturned
stones in our front yard.

And you're the lifelessness
underneath
that cannot reply.

Nowhere-Man

It's not located in the eyes, or the spine,
or the heart, but in the two hands—nails hacked, torn,
stress-bitten—and the draining brain.

It's clear. I'm jealous. A poet discusses her father's phone calls—
such inspiration—while unreliable flickers of Dad tease
my distant lobes. She says, *there's a poem everywhere.*
I say, *there's also a poem nowhere.*

It's true. I'm jealous. You're right; I'm left
alone, puzzled, puzzling
these razed patches of a man.
A mustache goes here. A bald spot goes there.

I carry a tin hand in mine; I start there—building, sculpting
a nowhere-man from a garbage heap. In there, only a single
Truth, from a pile of perfect ideas, can be assembled.

Sonnet for the Stones

He took the bills and stuck them in his sock
and said, *That damn social security*

is not enough to get us through the month.
My father shook his head, waved us goodbye,

and zoomed off in his car. The day went on,
men had come and gone, Grandpa's sock had filled.

A movie played real softly in the room
and Grandpa fell asleep right where he sat.

I went outside to chase squirrels in the yard,
but not until I found a couple stones

to stuff inside my socks, pretending they
were diamonds to be hoarded like a king.

But soon I saw the redness seeping through
and tossed the blood-soaked stones back in the grass.

The Fair

I have never become a town, though
the ghost-thought swimming in the streets
nips at my ears—never hammered
a city inside myself. As a child, I gathered

fairground buckeyes in my shirt,
like a drain hoarding marbles, and skipped
them off brick walls, morphing

tree orbs into moth wings
in my mind—to hope
something new would birth

from the debris below, to make
a collection multiply through explosion.

Yes, ants cluster around a molten dab of butter,

and will wage war to do so, but there is no
celebration in that. Here, we are crowds
smiling at crowds—occasionally wondering why

we are here and how respite zips at us
like flies. Perhaps wood and iron keeps
a soul sparked from a child's first night being

one in thousands—seeing the adults
toddler-wobble in tow—and the quiet of empty
cornfields staring in from the outside.

Grassman

I'm not supposed to believe
in the Grassman, that walking shag,
shambling Yggdrasil limb, soul of tree let loose.

The things seen with child
eyes in backyards on backroads
are, at the very best, unreliable—
I understand this.
And we humans snatch mind
lickers like web threads
tugging on ragweed frames—we distort and misplace
images by the landslide—and the bodies on deathbeds,
the fists sent through doors, the sobbing
on floors are dungeon-ghouls we shackle
to recession. The sponge that
stamps the top of our necks,
and its runny nature, is reason
enough for given pause.
It's true.
I may've misremembered.
I may've only glimpsed what I wanted
to see the most.
To this day, I've never again
witnessed a blade of grass dance
the way it did to me in that adolescent spring.
Science says no mossy rug
can grow veins and tendons
and roam the woods
in isolation. I know. I know. I know.

I'm not supposed to believe
in the Grassman, that peat specter,
dandelion tramp, beast of Mother Earth.

Yet, I do.

Sonnet for Innocence

A tower touches the sun, greenery
dampens below, as a boy sits atop

it like the star on a tree. God's given
him a spyglass to watch the world unfold

underneath him. It does. His mother and
father are young again, dancing in the

rain—a deer is born every second while
another dies curled up in rotting leaves—

birds take nosedives and fish swallow tadpoles
whole. With each glance through the glass

the tower's beams splinter; with each image
darting in the mist, the stone cracks. The boy

stops, holds the spyglass like the hand of a
loved one, and drops it from the window.

Beetle Song

Yes, of course, I say to the boy
as summer fevers the cement—burning
each child's foot while they scramble to snag
ants from the dirt—as a mother dances

with her daughter in the pool.
I see you, a sable
thumbprint, clamping onto the small
of the girl's back. I hear you slice your buzz
through the swarms of laughter.

A boy with grass-stains
on his knees calls out, *Do you think this is
real gold?* Another boy cries to God, asking why

he's never the one to find treasure.
In a memory, a beetle medallion is dangling in
the gypsy market when I am ten, when the Ohio

sun sieves through the tapestry-thin tent—I'm sure,
when the swaying woman draws near, kissing my
willowy cheek, its flaxen green
flickers in her pupil. *It's pure gold,* she tells me,
as my father sacrifices his wallet for my smile.

It is a birthmark that pecks
at my collar, a brand-burn on my neck—
until the chain inevitably breaks, and the yard
swallows it like a seed.

So, now, the mother brushes
you from her child like a spill
from a table, and you land
on my shoulder, humming secrets
into my ear.

The boy with filthy hands
pulls on the pocket of my
jeans—*Is this real gold?*

I remember asking my father
that same question years ago—a fleeting
Yes, of course bumbling off his tongue, and I feel
my father's voice jump through my teeth.

She said, "Lift."

I remember being told to soak
myself in unreason—that words
fall to pieces because the wind

needs her role; not everything
must be a weight to grunt over.

In you, amber formed to gem-
stones that I plucked and ate
like strawberries, that I carried

with promise—I floated in
the unlikeliest of ways—

your glass foaming inside
my throat. Moving forward
is pleasant when the belly

feels warm and full. Now, as change
calls, I am not Hasnah; I cannot

remove you from me in crystal
tears. I can only cough
a red glow up and drop

it on a star—each retch
an inch closer to Earth
receiving the soles of my feet,

a polished memory, though false,
laid neatly on a table.

Grandma Sonnet

The woods have eaten people, Grandma said.
A witch's hour ticks on every clock.

Why I'm never seen shoeless in the grass.
The sheets are filled with burn holes, cigarettes

left out like milk to spoil—musk that fills
your nose; those voices spill from my commode.

To be afraid of rabid chants that dance
on through the trees is sensible when you've

seen what I've seen. Now go ahead and play
amongst the bugs, eyes swiveled in the green.

Those men who hide around the bushes wait
for when your gaze is taken by the clouds.

And when you see them run inside to us—
lay next to me and we'll be safe and sound.

Song for Circe

Anna Marie Hahn was put to death on December 7th,
1938 in the Ohio State Penitentiary

Oh, Anna Marie,
     the Ohio grass was green
        the trees were
            green has died
    in your winter
       lightning strikes fork on
your temple tremors these Shawshank cornerstones
       fall to dirt
            shakes and groans in thirsting throats
    with your haunted hands squeezing
        like poisoned arteries
     in mazy hallways the Union soldiers drink gin
        gleefully
            pull on slots make them sing
of lonely men breaking skulls off cell bars you watched
      them squirm in old skin
          crinkling like fat globs of silver coins
Oh, Anna Marie,
    you incurve my sunken back
      with your fist, blacker

      than pupil spots—you stir
the kettle is warm with the philter
              your brew
       I have indulged in death meets me
   on you
I have kissed
      the pillow shivers
        I'm sweating for you I'm turning

      in my rind the blood curdles the toxins

    on your tongue I touch my own
Oh, Anna Marie,

I have no noose, nettle,
or scruple—I swallow

the obol chatters in my gums

      I taste the gold
hair falling from your scalp
           crosses out my eyes
      Oh, Circe

Oh, blackening
    Oh, goddess I am dead
        and you did it merrily
    danse macabre
      dancing bones in puddles of tar
              I'm sinking
I sniff the cup
wearily I gulp it down
      ordinarily I don't do this
    on the first date you drowned
      me in myself I see you black mist
        Oh, Anna Marie

black flag black sea I engorge
    on the sip
      at the tip of the glass I toast to you
        Death! Death! is a pretty
    face me do your worst
      of all you never cry
        you smile all the way
to the bank
    in the chair you twist
      you crackle
        as fire fills my chest I see you squarely
        you are beautiful you are still
  and your soul is bruised

The Cardinal's Song

He handed me a box of coins and said,
My father gave these to me long ago

and now I pass them on to you because
my mind will make me sell them all away.

He turned and left into his room to wait
on Grandma hand and foot—his name had bounced

through teeth and darted from the door. I took
the box and looked at all the shine—silver

reflected my small eyes. In them I saw
the twist of time and men who built what I've

never seen. In the woods, a cardinal sings
its songs as treasure chimed along with them.

You bastard! sounded loudly from the house
and when I flinched, my pockets filled with air.

The Bonfire

The trash, a mountain, poked the greying clouds—
my swings, the fort we built, now broken down

to burn. Your dolls. My army men. The kitchen set.
You're coughing cries and sweating hate. I see

him raging—Grandpa, drunk and breathing fire.
Like lightning bugs, the smoke hung all around

us—in a riot, Grandpa did his dance
and said, *You kids would never need to want*

when all you love is dust inside your lungs.
You took my hand and rushed me through the woods

and branches echoed-off his blackened laugh.
I spun with you and wished it all away;

among the deer is where we'll have to live
as pixies flutter through the dying leaves.

Song for the Neighborhood Girls

Behind the shed, she asked me,
            Can I see?
                  I didn't know
and nothing left my mouth. The house's bones
                  began to rattle like a snake.
The sky swelled up like Grandma's feet. She said,

                        *Don't worry, you can touch
            mine too.*
            The evening came. The clouds turned gray
                  with gloom.
Although the air was cracking
      booms, I stayed
            to drench my skin and let the rain
                  run down—the older neighbor girls
      ran back inside and left me all alone.

            I picked at bugs beneath a rock; my clothes
began to soak, while Grandpa's voice had bounced

            between the rain:
                  the fuck you doing, boy?

In seconds he grabbed me by my neck
                  and asked me *What the hell
                        is wrong with you?*
            I didn't know and my throat
                  clogged with words—
as thunder burst across the sky
            and lightning jigged within his eyes, softness
      grasped his face and God had touched
his shoulders—darkness rolled down his back,
                  past his ankles, and into the mud.

            Like a newborn on the teat, he carried
                  me inside.

Additional Acknowledgements:

Thank you to the North East Ohio Masters of Fine Arts program and Youngstown State University for funding my schooling, as well as giving me the opportunity to teach. Additionally, much appreciation is given to the extended NEOMFA cohort, past and present, for countless workshop hours.

Many thanks to Mary Biddinger, Catherine Wing, and Phil Brady for writing wonderful blurbs and for being great mentors. Additionally, thanks to Steve Reese for being a great resource and mentor. Thanks to Rochelle Hurt, Allison Pitinii Davis, Kenneth Patchen, and James Wright for being continuous sources of inspiration.

Thank you to my friends, who have helped me out tremendously in the last few years, Cassandra Lawton, McKayla Rockwell, Nathaniel Stokes, Tommy Mihalopoulos, Jack Ohliger, and others.

Lastly, thank you to my family: Mom, Miranda, Jeremy, Grandma, Aunt Phyl, Grandpa, etc. I cannot thank you enough for your support.

Dom Fonce is a poet from Youngstown, Ohio. He is the author of the two chapbooks *Here, We Bury the Hearts* and *Dancing in the Cobwebs.* He is an MFA candidate at the NEOMFA. His poetry has been published in *Gordon Square Review, Rappahannock Review, Delmarva Review, Obra/Artifact, Sweet Tree Review, Italian Americana, 3Elements Review, America's Best Emerging Poets 2018,* and elsewhere. He previously worked as Editor-in-Chief of *Volney Road Review.*